# Pangs of
# *The Heart*

Maudrey Zenon

Copyright © 2024 Maudrey Zenon
All rights reserved
First Edition

PAGE PUBLISHING
Conneaut Lake, PA

First originally published by Page Publishing 2024

ISBN 979-8-88793-433-4 (pbk)
ISBN 979-8-88793-440-2 (digital)

Printed in the United States of America

Dear Heavenly Father,

I dedicate this testimonial book to your precious Son, Jesus, and the sweet Holy Spirit! Your son, who was persecuted on His way to Calvary for the remission of our sins, bled, died, and was buried, but on the third day He rose from the grave with all power in His hands over hell, death, and the grave!

Thank you, Jesus!

May you work your magnificent miracles in the lives of the readers. May they be inspired to give their hearts, souls, and spirits to you then lean on you to live a holy and righteous life in your eyes! If I could do it with Jesus, so can you. God has no expectations of a person. What He does for one, He'll do for you!

Sister Maudrey Zenon

# Part 1

Say what?

Another person has gone to the voodoo doctor, and from the computer, God told me who it was. It was hard to believe, so I kept asking Him, "God, did she really go?"

God keep telling me, "Yes, Maudrey. I know how you feel defenseless, but I'm God, and you know my voice!"

"But why oh why could she have done something so cruel that makes number four-two dead and two living?"

"Maudrey, you lashed out at her with a loud voice for disturbing your peace at home with a bunch of verbal nonsense she said in her heart."

"You'll never holler at me again!"

I remember when the evidence of voodoo all started. My tongue hurt so bad, it was like someone branded it with a hot iron shaped like a circle. I had to go to my medical doctor and she ordered me a special mouthwash. After a week, it got well. Cupcake didn't want me to talk though. One day, I told my oldest granddaughter to bring my two rocks that I had in a box from Cupcake's garage. God gave them to me in Lake Charles, Louisiana. The smaller one, He said, was my academy award because I acted out a certain Christian skit at a Wendy's restaurant.

The larger rock God told me to pick it up from the sidewalk, so I did, but I didn't know why. When I got to my apartment, I asked God what the oval-shaped rock meant.

"Jesus said everything I've told you and everything I've showed you are concrete." Then my eyes became spiritually open. "It was a concrete rock from the ruins of the old Sears department store downtown parking lot!" My friend was coming to visit me in Lafayette, Louisiana, for the Easter week. I told her to please bring my rocks, and she did.

Well, one day after my friend was gone, I was looking up at the hutch where my decorations were, and I noticed my rock looked different and frightening. I stared at the rocks for a while, and I saw it for what it was.

The rock had the face of a snake! I became afraid. Jesus told me to put some gloves on my hands then pitch that in the streets. I didn't want to touch it, gloves or not, but I did what Jesus told me. I live at a dead end, so I just threw it as far as I could in the street. My neighbor picked the rock up and put it in a trash bin the maintenance men were using for old debris from an empty apartment. A couple of days later, I was straightening up my bed, but I was making it up a little messy. The day after that, I was really making up the bed accurately. As I was pulling on the sheet at the corners, much to my surprise, I saw a large imprint of a cobra snake with a big round head and an S-shape body!

I was very upset, but I didn't cry. All I could think about was, *Who did this?*

I immediately pulled the sheet off of the bed, and I put it in the trash. Dre had just bought me that sheet when she came down from Atlanta, Georgia. I sure didn't want it anymore! About three to four days after, Cupcake called my phone. She hadn't talked to me for about two months because of my outburst (you know, when someone calls you on the phone, you say hello, then you get a rapid response). Cupcake didn't give me a rapid response. She waited to hear what my voice was going to sound like.

She was looking for a depressed and frightful response from me. After about fifteen seconds of silence, she excitedly said, "Oh, Maudrey." That's how she address me. "What are you going to do with your stuff in my garage? I was supposed to move to Atlanta, Georgia, a couple of years ago, but I changed my mind."

I told her to give it all to Goodwill, then she hurried and said, "Okay." Then she hung up the phone. She doesn't know I knew what she was doing!

A couple of nights after that, Jesus was sitting by my bedside. Before I opened my eyes, three snakes fell to the floor. In my mind, when I opened my eyes, Jesus had taken a brand-new throw blanket I had never unwrapped. He got it out of the hutch cabinet door. Jesus had it folded in two sections, and it was already placed on top of my shoulders to my waist! I asked Jesus why did He do that, and He responded, "It was a chest protector!" The blanket fell to the floor at the same time I opened my eyes. Nothing else was said about it before Jesus left. He took the long gray ribbed ribbon from the throw blanket and tied it in a bow on the knobs of the hutch in the living room in my small efficiency apartment. About a week after that, I kept feeling like serpents, cold and wet, were moving around on my right arm, thigh, and leg.

What am I to do, scream? I don't think so; people would ask what's wrong. I couldn't say that I feel snakes on the right side of my body! I just cried out to God every day, "Please help me and take that away." Today is October 26, 2021, and I'm still feeling the same way! Since September 2021, "Please help me, God!"

I sure can't tell the doctors—you know what they would do to me! Can you imagine the medicine or the dosage? I'll just keep it to myself! Before I released this horrific story to you, Jesus had to talk to my face. It's Saturday, the thirtieth of October 2021, and Jesus didn't talk to my face, but He definitely made a believer out of me after He deleted everyone whom I thought it could be. The only one who was standing out was Cupcake.

Jesus is coming back to my house, and I will see Him face to face. He's going to escort my husband to be to me! At first, Jesus was in my apartment in spirit, but next time, He will let me see Him face to face to heal me! The other reason is because I read Apostle David E. Taylor's book *Face to Face Appearances*. Jesus has been visiting him quite frequently ever since David was eighteen years young, and everyone who reads his book will get a face-to-face visitation from Jesus!

God knows when Jesus comes. I believe I'll be alright if it's after He's gone. I'm worried that the devil will make me have a battle in my mind, that Jesus wasn't real and that's why my husband-to-be, Dr. Marcus Love, will forever be by my side. No more worries, lies, heartaches, or nervous breakdowns. I'll have my own personal psychiatrist.

Thank you, Jesus! From the verves to the curves!

Girl, if what you did made you happy or satisfied in anyway, so be it.

I feel sorry for you, I still forgive and will always love you!

But because of the demonic ordeal you put me through, it has to be done from a long handle spoon!

I told you, "A Mother's Love Never Dies" was sung by one of my favorite gospel singers, the late great Brother Lee Williams! I want everyone to know I forgive everybody!

The kidnappers!

The backstabbers!

The heartbreakers

and the liars!

My family who put me on the back burner, my sisters who never visited me at my many apartments, my uncle Voorhies, who turned his back on me because I was sick, I apologized to everyone! Those who befriended me then left me high and dry because of their own insecurities, my son, Christian, who spat in my face one day, it shocked the hell out of me, but I purposed in my heart that that wasn't my son! That was the devil who did that!

My daughter Cupcake who went to the devil for me!

My baby Malcolm would never have hurt me, he'd rather get run over by a Mack truck! Then my stepson, whom I call my son, his name is Brandon Bell and he loves me unconditionally. He likes for me to make him laugh!

Nothing will stop me from loving my children, whether they do right or wrong!

I love you, little Brian Victorian. I call you my son too!

Those who loved me when they saw me far and between, but when I was out of ya'll sight, I was out of mind! I love you cousins Monica B. Rubin and Millie Jones, then Gloria King and Aunt Tee. Lorita Benoit, y'all stood till the end! Sick or not, my friends from Genesis, I'm on a road of new beginnings with Jesus, Marcus, and the ones who truly love me!

Thank you, Sister Maudrey.

# Part 2

April 15, 2021

To all the expectant mothers who's pondering with a satanic desire to do away with the innocent embryos you're carrying, please reconsider! I know we may think we've won the war when we do something so horrific, but we've only won the battle. I know that I know I've been forgiven by God, Jesus, and myself. I was even told, "The baby forgives me too."

How beautiful it is.

Sometimes, the uncontrollable memory walks across my mind and wounded heart every now and then! I can't do anything but weep. It's not a cry of desolation or repentance because I've done that forty plus years ago. I just would like to see my baby and let him know I love him!

That's the reason I wanted to make this serious plea for all babies to be spared and loved in the womb! I'm free now! I've come to know the power of God's amazing grace and forgiveness! Thanks for taking the time to read my article because it's straight from my heart and soul!

Sister Maudrey
Cell: 337-602-0072

Come and let us reason together if you need me!

My Heavenly Father told me to sign all of my work with *Queen of Heart*.

To Sister Sandra Zenon,

Oh how I wished I had the tenacity she had in her spiritual walk with Jesus! In that, I mean she was sixty plus years old, but not one time did anyone of her eight sisters see or hear her murmur and complain about her physical condition.

At birth, the doctor told our mother Sandra that she won't live past the age of six years old. As we can see, it's not up to any man—doctor or not!

She was special when she was born. She was blind in one eye, and she had polio. Plus, because of the removeable blind eye, her right arm and hand drew back during surgery.

Ma kept Sandra under her thumb, so to speak. She wouldn't go out the front door to live and explore life like we did!

She worked at CARC for a very long time until she couldn't anymore. She always sat quietly in the living room with Ma. I often wondered what was going on in her mind and heart as she was expressionless. She watched us day in and day out experiencing our facets of life! My heart ached for her!

Then one day, her health changed. She was confined to the bed for several years! One thing I know, Sandra eagerly said the sinner's prayer one afternoon with me.

A very, very long time ago, that same night at dinner while she was eating, I literally saw the Shekina glory of God confirming her acceptance to Jesus. The sign was shining both in her face and it was hovering over the top of her head! The only way I can describe it was that the appearance was like a light purple color of smoke!

Hallelujah!

Not only was she an inspiration to me, but she was the epitome of faith, love, and the Holy Ghost's power! She had a great home going.

Gloria, King!

I love your name, it's so spiritual. You're my bestest, bestest friend in the whole wide world.

She's more like my blood sister. I call her my "million dollar" friend. We tell each other everything, and she'll do anything within her power for me!

We've been friends since 1983. No matter where we lived, our motto was, "My house is your house." I truly mean it, she feels my pains and joy, and me, hers.

Cloudy days, rainy days, or sunny days, we are always the same. Most times, we're feeling the same way!

The best thing of all, we love to shoot the breeze about anything, and we have the same sense of humor. Boy!

The fun we have is great, and by the way, her cooking is hard to beat, but her love you really need to meet!

She'll give you the shirt off her back. When she does, be sure you cover up though, but don't cover up your caring, sharing, and your laugh.

You stuck by me through the good, bad, and the ugly—when everybody else rejected me for jealous reasons.

But not you, Gloria. I'll never forget that you were like Jesus. You stuck by me closer than a brother or sister, literally!

We took a licking, but we kept on ticking. Stay sweet and loving just like you are.

Marge

7-1-2021

Prisoner in My Own Heart!

When will someone unlock the door and let me out? I've been confined for forty plus years in pain and misery, hurting from lack of attention and affection, dying on the inside hiding behind a smile.

I was married twenty-two years, but that doesn't count. I married for money, so the love was only one way, his way. I'll tell anyone please don't settle if it's not mutual! It's like being in a crowded room, and you still feel empty and alone! I loved him but I wasn't "in love"!

My so-called friends, the few I had, abandoned me because they couldn't understand or cope with the idea I was older than them, but looked a whole lot younger than they did!

My sisters were always there to take me to the hospital when I became sick. To the stores as well but when that chore was done, I was done. I cried many, many days for their affection and respect. Because I was the oldest there were no phone calls and no visits in my home. Oh, how that hurt me to the core of my heart. No invites to the weekends and no get togethers. I just wanted to be with them because they make me laugh!

Every now and then I would call them, but they would screen the calls to see what I wanted, and if they answer they would say, "What's up?" As far as I'm concerned, rude!

I've been anticipating my future husband for nine years in divorce years, but four prior to that when I left my late husband!

How welcome and refreshing that will be to me! I even picked out his name. I want it to be Doctor Marcus Love! Marcus means "copy our Christian life style and you can be blessed like us!" Love means God is love! I love you and you're supposed to love!

Our love will be so strong, irresistible, and inseparable that no devil from hell will prevail against it! God said that He bottled up my tears. Trust me, it was a lot. He's going to give me beauty for my ashes! Joy, joy, joy unspeakable!

The only true love I had was from my two sons, Malcolm and Christian, my three beautiful granddaughters, and my two play sons, Brandon and Little Brian. My only grandson, Messiah Christian Zenon, was taken out of my arms when he was about four months old and nobody looked back for me to be in his life! It disgusted me that his mom gave him to a homosexual couple. Yes they took good care of him, but I didn't and don't want him to grow up confused a one-year-old baby. He was even younger, he can only say da-da and mommy! They reside in Houston,

Texas, and the name of the woman who's playing his mom is Marquel Speight.

To finish my story, my two biological sons stayed in jail. Perpetually their physical love was taken away from me for decades then my oldest son got strung out on drugs. He was homeless for seven years and now he's in the streets of New Orleans fighting demons of addiction! Many Christians are sending up prayers for all of them to the throne of God.

My baby boy is in prison in Cottonport, LA. By the way, he doesn't like me calling him that he comes out in 2022, but God says he's coming out early. Chris did a few months in Angola State Penitentiary just because he told an officer something when he was angry! My son Brandon is doing time in prison in Tallulah, LA. He gets out in 2028. My other play son, Little Brian, I don't know where he is right now!

My daughter and my three beautiful granddaughters, Eladria, Shanti, and Imani, weren't always on the forefront in terms of faith and love. For fourteen years, my daughter kept them from me simply because I chose to take a rent-free home for eighteen months in Oklahoma for Hurricane Rita, so I missed seeing them grow up.

On top of that, they live four states from me! As you can see, I have a lot on my plate. It's choking me! I cry out to God for His mercy and goodness to free this enslaved heart of disappointments and heartaches! I'm human too. I long for a hug, a kiss, a dance, a smile etc. No special order, all in the matchless name of Jesus! God told me one day, "Maudrey, if I call you daddy's little girl and my princess, can't you trust me to give to you your heart's desire?"

I'm sorry, Dad. Blame my mind not my heart. I love and believe wholeheartedly. It's just the times the devil is against me!

Even the Bible says in Genesis 2:18, it's not good for man to be alone—that means married or single! I pray it back to God all the time!

I know that I know this is my season because God wants to give you more than what you can handle right now. I feel that's an "understatement." It was prophesied about four years ago that "God wants me to struggle a little while longer and it will benefit me and my family," so I said, okay Lord! Now I'm saying, how long is a little while?

On Tuesday, August the 10th, 2021, when I got out of the shower and entered the living room, much to my surprise, God had shined everything in the whole small apartment. When I say everything, that's what I mean, from the bibles to the tiles on the floors! That was the biggest sign ever and it was with holy oil!

## MAUDREY ZENON

I truly believe this is the beginning of something big, like fireworks on the Fourth of July in my heart!

I'm getting ready to walk through open doors of love, joy, and happiness forever and a day this year, 2021.

8-12-2021

> Joy cometh in the morning!
>
> —Psalm 30:5

Who is Sister Maudrey?

First of all, I must say, "I'm just a nobody trying to tell everybody about someone who can save anybody."

I said "someone" because there's no other option! I'm a born-again believer who loves the Lord with all my heart, soul, and strength. I have a strong desire in my heart to see everyone saved and filled with the Holy Spirit. Yes, I know God enlarged hell for nonbelievers who rejects Jesus Christ, our Redeemer.

If people don't obey God's holy word, who am I? I'm just an ambassador for Jesus Christ. God doesn't want to see anyone go to hell, but know that He's not sending you there. Your rebellious spirit and hardened heart to His word and commandments does that. You make the choice to go to heaven or hell. God loves everyone, but He doesn't like sin.

He sent His only begotten Son to die on the cross. He was buried and He rose on the third day!

He took every sin imaginable upon Himself, as we were yet sinners, to give us access to heaven when we pass to the other side and freedom from all the strongholds of

Satan on this side, while trying to win souls to Christ while we have a chance to!

Many turn their hearts, heads, and ears the opposite way of righteousness! So who is wrong here? The wage of sin is still death! The gift of God is eternal life. Don't say God is not a good God because He is, and no one is exempted from trials and tribulations! So don't hate Him because someone wasted away, young or old. This is not our home, but Jesus gives, and the devil steals, kills, and destroys. I believe God still has the final say. "Look at Job." I'm an old-fashioned country girl from Duson, Louisiana, about nine miles in front of Lafayette, Louisiana, where I reside at this moment because of Hurricane Laura. This is not my final destination though!

My mom moved to Lake Chares, Louisiana, when I was five years young. I did twelve years of schooling here but to be honest, even though I graduated in 1969 at W. O. Boston High, I didn't apply myself in school. That's why my walk in life was hard and broken. In school, my many friends allowed me to copy off their papers, test time or not, so nothing stuck on my brain. To be truly honest with you and myself, grades 1 to 3 I thought I was smart. Grades 4 to 12, I was dependent on my peers' intelligence. All I enjoyed were milk breaks, recess, PE, lunch, and home economics! All I wanted to be in life was a housewife with three children and a loving husband till death did us part (you don't need an education for that)!

Like my grandmother, Adell Jones Zenon, Aunt Lorita, her daughters Monica and Stephanie, and a few others, I graduated from Job Corps in Guthrie, Oklahoma, as a keypunch operator and a PBX operator. I did my on-job training on and off the center. I spent three months in Manhattan, New York City, but worked in Brooklyn, New York, at a navy finance company. I graduated in the winter of 1970. I traveled to many cities, but I've always found myself back home where my heart was. My mind kept telling me I wanted to be where the bright lights were. Because of the sin in my life, things didn't go as I hoped. It would be at age seventeen after high school graduation, that's when my mind was introduced to the spirits of discouragement and despair! I didn't know what to do with myself. That snowballed for a half of a century. Happiness for me was very, very few and far between. The spirit of darkness hovered over my mind and heart for a long extended time. One day, when I was in the backseat of a kidnapper's car in 1971, I sincerely said in my heart, "God, if you get me out this mess I'm in, I'll serve you all the days of my life!" How many made that confession and didn't keep it? Well, I didn't. I was still young, restless, and twenty years young. I quickly forgot about what God had done for me. When I had enough of doggy dog days of doom and gloom in my life, I fell on my knees and became born-again all over, if that's such a thing. I felt dirty and soiled on the inside. Like they say, you've tried everything else, now try Jesus!

I was baptized several times too. I'm not saying that applies to you, it was something I wanted to do. Water baptism doesn't save you, it just symbolizes Jesus's death, burial, and resurrection! I'm steadfast and unmovable in God's word, mercy, and grace! He kept me when I couldn't keep myself. Somebody prayed for me like the song says. Without a shadow of doubt, God delivered me from many satanic snares and plans the devil had to disintegrate my life. I'm totally rooted and grounded in righteousness. I must say, all the times I was in the sanctuary praising and worshipping Jesus, that was my refuge and haven; nothing can touch me there. I've even gotten sick sometimes in the church parking lot after service.

I want to be a spiritual counselor. You know what they say, "experience is the best teacher." I just want God to use me and my offspring in any way He sees fit. After the numerous trial and errors (and that's an understatement) in my life, I just want to reach out to someone in love and concern because I'm truly free indeed!

By the way, I'm licensed by the Holy Spirit, if anyone wants to know! See you at my desk in my office or at the box office!

Love you all in Jesus's name!

Sister Maudrey

"Queen of Heart"

P.S. The movie will explain all that and more!

Cell: 337 602 0072

Maudrey means "mother."
Zenon means "friendly."

# MAUDREY ZENON

Sister Maudrey, sixty-seven years young.

I just wanted to show ya'll I don't look like where I've been!

Amen.

Picture taken in 2019.

Forgive me if I offended anyone with my photo.

I just have an aura of sexiness, but I'm a sold-out woman of God!

I didn't count the cost!

I was married for twenty-two years, but that was the worst time of my life! I gave all of my young years to my husband. I loved him, but I wasn't in love with him. His name was Ervin. He did everything that he could to make me happy. The more he bought, the more I took that, yes, I would be happy for a while, but when it was time to pay the piper, I hated it. When it was daytime, we got along fine. When he would get off of work, he would take a bath then he would always take me and my two sons, who are his "Christian and Malcolm," riding in the car to buy ice cream or snow cones—anything we wanted in the nearby towns. Ervin was always trying to put a smile on our face. When I got tired of pretending with our relationship, I had to get out! I used to tell him, "I'm not your wife, I'm your prostitute!" That's how I felt in my heart! I tried and tried to make it right in my soul, but I couldn't. I would even pray to God to make me feel just some of what Ervin feels. To be honest with you, that's how we started our relationship. I wasn't working, and I needed to get my four-year-old daughter's layaway out for her to get a head start.

The layaway was one hundred dollars. I didn't see any other way when I submitted to that act. I cried liked a baby! I can't even describe how I felt when he did his business well. He gave me the hundred dollars then left. He stayed away for a couple of weeks, and I purposed in my heart to do the same thing again because I was somewhat lazy. I didn't mind getting furniture, cars, money, etc. on my back! It was humiliating for me to be seen with him. He didn't mind, so I didn't either! He loved me to the fullest until his heart was running over with admiration. I used to tell him to give some of that love to Jesus! When I tried to witness to him, he tried to rape me!

When you don't love something, you'll treat it any kind of way. Before we were married, I would take him in the house for payday, throw him out on Wednesday, then pick him up on payday again, and I wouldn't have a second thought of remorse!

Well, lo and behold, I got mentally tired of our so-called marriage, I got a divorce. I left Ervin and went to live with my girlfriend, but I was praying to God for a Christian husband. I thought it was going to come fast because I left an equally yoked marriage.

God spoke to my spirit and said, "Mauredy, I can't bless you with a husband because you are still tied up in a marriage license." Immediately, I called the legal aid office, but there were specific rules to get through. Well, I went on and I got an apartment in Sulphur, Louisiana, about nine or ten miles from Lake Charles. After a year there, I left and went to Atlanta, Georgia, where my daughter and grandchildren live. While there, I received a phone call that my husband had a massive stroke and he was in a nursing home. His family took him to a little town call Mamou, Louisiana. After a couple years there, he was brought to Lake Charles, Lousiana. I would go visit him daily until he started talking under my clothes. I would tell him that door is shut by the Holy Spirit, and I'll never enter it again!

He would always talk about how he was tired of being in the nursing home, so one day, I signed him out and brought him to my apartment in Lake Charles. I spoke to my rent man, and he was going to give Ervin an apartment. I knew my baby boy, I call him that, but he's a man who was going to be getting out of jail in a week, so all by myself I took care of Ervin who was deadweight. The nurse didn't give me what you call a gait belt till later. Anyway, it was on a Tuesday evening, about 7:00 p.m., Ervin said in a nonchalant way, "Maudrey, you abuse me."

I excitedly reply, "What you mean?" He just laughed. I was very angry at him. I thought to myself, *If he doesn't appreciate me, I'm taking him back to the home.* Lo and behold, he said it again on the next Tuesday. I quickly told him, "Tomorrow, I'm sending you back to the nursing home." He laughed at me, but I was serious as a heart attack. The next morning, his provider came, and as soon as she sat down, Ervin burst out in a cry, telling the lady I was sending him back to the home. Well, she called the police. They were judging me, saying, "Isn't a marriage till death do us part?"

I said, "Yes, when both are in love."

Ervin died a few years ago. God bless his soul, to wrap this up. I'll admit the same thing I told Ervin when he bought me anything, I felt like a lady of the evening. The only difference was, I was in my home and not on the streets. The one good thing that came out the end of our relationship, I repented to him and I repented to God for being ugly to Ervin!

I went to God to pick out my Christian husband. Not only that, I want him to be a psychiatrist! It's been more than twelve years I've been waiting!

I'm a sweet, gentle, kind, loyal woman. I took the wrong path in my early years, and I stayed longer than I wanted to stay! I paid more than I wanted to pay! In the end, I'll say if you're a Christian, do the right thing from the beginning! If you're not, it's time to get right! Get saved!

My life is wholeheartedly dedicated to the Lord. Whatever He wants me to do, I'll do and wherever He wants me to go, I'll go.

God knows my shortcomings based on my experiences of the kidnapping in my past. I'll feel more secure or protected with my intended husband by my side, working together like in the Bible two by two in Jesus's name.

**MAUDREY ZENON**

*Pangs of The Heart*—God told me to write this story, and I have one final story to write about me meeting the Christian man God picked out for me.

Maudrey, prayerfully real soon.

# A Sinner Saved by Grace! The Way We Were—1975

I wrote a very long story about my first secret rendezvous with my daughter's daddy. If I may be honest, in the late 1999, I had a short romantic interlude with a thug while I was married. You know what they say, a fling with a thug is like a bug in the rug. He not only makes you feel young, he makes it darn good because he doesn't know when it will be his next time around. Like the song says, "It's good when you're stealing it." You do know that's a bunch of hog wash? God told me after two months' time in the adultery affair to cut it off, so I did. I didn't want to buy him cigarettes, beer, and weed anymore. Anyway, we seasoned women know how the game is played! Back to 1975, I met this very handsome blind date. I fell deeply in love at first sight. My feelings got away from me before I could retrieve them back. His name was Hunter. He loved me too, but he wasn't man enough to hold up his part of the relationship even though he was shacking with another woman. I had no idea if he still loved me, but I know even if he weren't,

I wasn't the one to buy his love like the three women he married after me!

Anyway, we had a good time dancing, romancing, going to the movies, etc. When I returned to Houston, Texas, when my daughter was about five months old, we picked up where we left off a year prior. That's when I found out, well he told me, he was married and his wife had a son almost at the same time of my baby's birth. I was devastated and hurt that he didn't play out my fantasy of marrying me! Yes, I was surprised and hurt after Hunter told me of his hidden secret. I went and licked my wounds for a few days. The love in our hearts couldn't keep us apart. It was like two peas in a pod, we were inseparable. He couldn't keep up with trying to love two, so he broke it up with me. Again and again, I went home in Lake Charles hurt, wounded, and sad, setting a bad example for my eight sisters to follow. It took me several years to get over Hunter. Early on, I wanted to commit suicide. You want to end things that's going bad, but the reality is, you will be beginning things that you can't get out of, such as hell. God gives you life, and He's the only one who can end it. Yes, the devil steals, kills, and destroys, but God has the final say! Look at the story of Job. If God hadn't stopped me, I was going to kill the baby inside me, which I had no clue of! That's why I know God speaks to everyone who wants to commit such an act. The question is, which voice are you listening to?

Without a shadow of a doubt, I know I was made for Hunter. After all the bull crap in my life, my heart, commitment, and love belongs to the man of God who God picks out for me. I want his name to be Minister Marcus Love, MD. All of my supernatural blessings are just upon the horizon! I'm too through with mess. I'm ready to be blessed!

Some people saved or unsaved may wonder why I wrote this raw testimonial book. Number 1, life is real and raw preachers all over the world of the Fivefold Ministry are preaching from the King James Bible. The principle of living holy, the pews are full of people, but are the people full of the principle? That is the question.

It still is holiness or hell, the choice is yours! The book is my testimony to whomever wants to receive it. I made lots of mistakes in my life, and I just don't want anyone to go through the ordeals I went through. Like I tell my four sons, two from another mother, y'all better recognize the devil's tactics before he gets too close to you and ruins your life!

Number 2, most of the subjects I speak about are the same things the preachers are telling us not to do, but in a biblical way.

The preachers of all different kinds are working very hard with blood, sweat, and tears, pleading from their hearts and soul for us, the people of all kinds, to live a clean life in order to make heaven a home! Are you listening and obeying? I am, the Bible says. If you love me, you'll keep my commandments. One last statement, I'm not judging anyone because that's not my call. Like the Bible, I just want to point you in the right direction—peace.

# *Repent*

To all who read my testimonial book, the just as well as the unjust, I have a deep desire in my heart that everyone become saved and born again! God enlarged hell because many will choose not to be holy and take the broad road to destruction, but that's not the heart of God. So here is my plea that everyone will accept and follow God's holy word to a greater life in the thereafter and even for today!

In Jesus's matchless name,
Sister Maudrey

# About My Father's Business!

Luke 2:49

Repent ye all, for the kingdom of heaven is at hand! If you don't know how, confess with your mouth that Jesus Christ is Lord then ask God our heavenly Father to forgive you of your sin! Believe in your heart the message of the cross, the great salvation plan that Jesus, the Son of God, was crucified and He shed His precious blood for the remission of our sins! On the cross He was buried, but on the third day, He rose from the grave with all power in His hands! Then ask Jesus to come live in your heart, that you may have peace in your soul and that He may rule and guide you. Then it's imperative that you live holy! Most people from the pulpit don't elaborate on this enough!

It's holiness or hell! The Bible says, "Be doers of His word and not hearers." "The icing on the cake" is being baptized in the Holy Spirit with the evidence or speaking in the holy language because that's what will keep and hold you in righteousness!

So I say, live holy.

Be holy.

Do holy!

This means meet your neighbor's need when possible. Then with a pure heart and a right spirit and when you've become absent from the body and present with the Lord, you shall be with Jehovah, God, and His beloved Son, seated at the right side of the heavenly Father on high!

Remember, no man can come to the Father except through Jesus!

This message is known as being born-again, saved, and sanctified!

John 3:16
Romans 10:9–10

## If I May Interject

You know God could have made abortion an unpardonable sin, especially with millions of innocent babies being mutilated and destroyed every twenty-four hours? The Bible says, "Blasphemy of the Holy Spirit is destroying God's perfect and wonderfully made creations in His image." Life could have been unforgiveable, but it wasn't "thank God" for His goodness grace and mercy! I just pray women wouldn't use that as a form of birth control. Oh, my Heavenly Father is so sweet and so kind. My soul bursts with excitement in His awesome love! That's why I told you one of my deepest darkest sins. Even though no one sin is greater than the least, it's all the same!

I wanted to save at least one mother's child, if not many, and if I did by posting an article about my abortion in January 22, 2018, Lake Charles, Louisiana, American Press edition on that date!

To God be the glory!

Remember, doing such an act, you may have won the battle, but you don't win the war. No matter how much you forgive yourself, the memory is always lurking in your heart.

# Can I Really Pay to Know the Future? Of Course Not

One last thing before I close the chapters in this book. In 2010, mediums flooded my mailbox with their advertisements I never signed up for. They just came and went. Back in 2003, I went to Sister Dianne in Eunice, Lousiana, when I lived in Crowley, Lousiana. I only went because of her name. I thoughted she was my sister in Christ.

I wanted my intended husband by any means, like God needed my help. Well upon arrival, Dianne walked us to a back room in her very large home. We sat down and in two seconds, she asked when I was fee, then she asked, "You, why are you here?" Then whatever you tell her, she tells it back to you in a subtle way. When you were through talking, she would give you a small sack of red pepper and salt mixture to throw under your bed before retiring for the night. Well, what can I say? I gave it a shot, it didn't work, and will never work. The palm readers, the psychic's hotline, and tarot cards are all satanic. Don't waste your time or your money.

My brother in Christ, whose name is Donald, brought me to Dianne, and on the second trip there, she pointed to Donald while he quietly sat in the corner of the room. "She says, why don't you marry him?" What? He was just my ride. Remember, she gets her money up front, so she didn't care. I got upset. I paid a small lump sum for her to tell me that crap!

When we were leaving, I asked Donald, "Why didn't you tell me she was a crook?"

He quickly replied, "You were the one who insisted on going there." Now I'm telling you don't fall for the okey dokey. Save your money and time. Jesus can fix anything that's broken and mend it back together with love and expertise! So wait and trust the Lord!

2018

I was admitted into the hospital from the emergency room, with pains that felt like contractions in my heart. Since I wasn't having a physical heart attack but I was in distress, the doctor kept me for overnight observation. Meanwhile, I was in constant pain. The doctors and nurses didn't know what to do with me. The next morning, I was wheeled into this room with a very large machine hanging from the ceiling. The tech took all kinds of pictures of my heart.

They didn't tell me anything until much, much later in that evening. The nurse came into the room and told me I had a fairly good heart and they couldn't find anything wrong with the pictures the machine had taken. I told her, "My heart may be good, but I'm hurting like hell," with tears in my eyes. Nobody knew what to do. Later on, about 3:00 p.m., old man Doctor Turner, a heart specialist, came by my bedside. He checked me over, and I told him the same thing. "I feel like I'm having a baby in my heart."

I don't know what pill he gave me, but it was like magic at about 9:00 p.m. The second night, I was totally relieved from all pain, and I went home the next day after lunch. After four decades of loneliness, even though I was married for twenty-two years, I suffered with heartaches, disappointments, mental illness, and backstabbing people calling me crazy behind my back. I feel my heart broke down emotionally. I'm good now, purged from powers of darkness that had me bound. It's covered by the blood of Jesus! The moral of the story is, don't try to carry the load of everyday life on your shoulders. Rest in Jesus and give it all to Him. He's the heavy load carrier, the burden barrier, the deliverer, and the lily of the valley, but most of all, the Savior!

The bright and morning star, He's our friend in all kinds of trouble!

Sister Maudrey

I want to add that my five sisters who were at my aunt's eighty years birthday party were very loving and respectful of me. Because my birthday was the following Monday the twelfth, the birthday bash was on the tenth. They showered me with money and cards. Thank you all, family. It was nice and joyful to see all of you!

I love you all, and may I add, I've genuinely loved the entire family since I was knee-high to a duck! Smile!

Let me not forget Eladria Jacore and Imani's bouquet of flowers and that my cousin, Millie Jones, gave me five balloons with a card and twenty dollars.

Thank all of you!

Some readers may ask, "Why is she putting all her business in a book form?" Number 1, that's all covered by the blood of Christ, and that's what I want for you. Stop the sin and win with Jesus. I'm not doing anything what the preachers of old used to ask of everyone not to do. Now majority of them are just preaching about prosperity.

Well, how does it prosper a man to gain the whole world and lose their soul? Those who want to get to heaven, read on. Number 1, you must repent (be sorry for your sins). Ask Jesus to come into your heart. Be baptized (be dunked) in the water then live holy each day the best you know how with the Holy Spirit as your guide!

Let me not forget, you must be baptized in the Holy Spirit with the utterance of speaking in tongues.

Amen.

PS Let the redeemed of the Lord say so, and that's what I'm doing!

# A Shout Out!

To all my pastors, prophets, and prophetesses past and present

To all my friends and family, especially my sisters who loved me and respected my seventy-first birthday on September 10, but my birthday is September 12.

A special shout-out to my cousin Millie Jones, RN, and her mom, Rose Jones. My old school road dog, she never changed with me and Millie never left my side in Lafayette, Louisiana.

A shout-out to Aunt Tee Lorita Benoit and her daughter, Monica Ruben! My strong Christian friends, Josephine Richard, and Shemika in Lake Charles, Louisiana, I love all of you!

# PANGS OF THE HEART

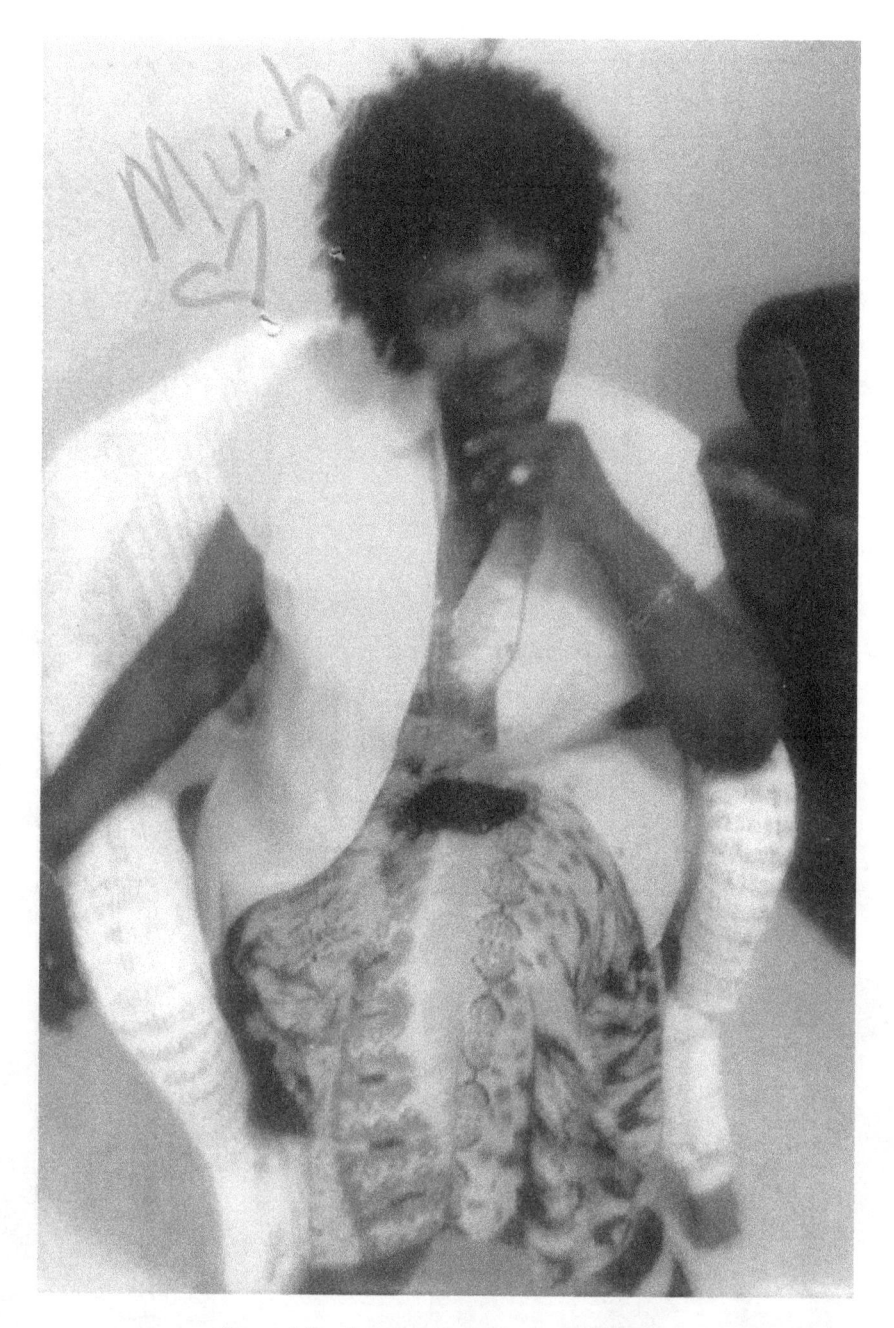

Sister Maudrey at sixty-two years young.

# MAUDREY ZENON

Big Marge!

Dear readers,

This book is inspired by the Holy Trinity! I spent many decades of dark doom and gloom, spirits that grasped my mind day in and day out, no special order and the only place I felt safe in was the refuge of the sanctuary where praise, worship, and preaching were going on!

I can't really explain my sickness. God has to do that, and He will in a movie. People always ask me if the kidnappers raped me. No, I'll say, they did that to my mind! When I was sick, it was as if my mind left me and went somewhere to hell, but God said that my love for Him, family, and friends would always bring me back to myself with medication! Be on the lookout for the movie. It simply will be called, *Sister Maudrey.*

# An Apology

First I want to apologize because all my original topics got lost in some kind of way in these stories I wrote in the latter days of 2021–2022.

A Shout-Out
To my seven sisters:
Baby girl and family
Patricia Richard
And Lakken
Pam the Ham (Pamela Trimpey)
Linda Ann and family
Brenda White (Carmen)
Melody Frances and family
And my cousin Darlene from Port Arthur, Texas
Love y'all!

# I Turned the Other Cheek

One summer day, I was sitting quietly on the sofa at my sister-in-law's house, looking at the television, when my oldest son, Christian Von, came in the house and walked past me then turned around and spit in my face. I was so shocked. I didn't say anything. I was bewildered for a minute or two.

I went outside to collect my thoughts. In my heart, I said, "That wasn't my son that did such a degrading thing to me. That was the devil."

Then I called my sister Melody. She's the one everybody looks to for answers. She immediately came with two big nephews. Terry jumped out of the SUV, came to the front door, and called Chris outside. He asked him, "Why did you spit in your mom's face?" Before he could answer, Terry sucker-punched him with a left hook, and he fell to the ground.

I was so happy. I was jumping six feet off the ground with cheers. Christian ran down the street. Both Dontrell and Terry ran after him, but Chris got away shortly after that scene. My birthday came up. Chris gave me two hundred dollars, then he said, "Look, Mom, I tattooed your name on my neck.

I responded with "I don't care if you tattooed your testicles. I'm not going to forgive you!"

Eventually time passed. I forgave my baby 'cause I love him!

Christian, I'm sorry I had to tell that story, but God is number one in my life, then y'all!

He was prophesied at three years young to be a preacher! Go figure.

(When Chris ran, Melody called the cops. They took him to jail but released him the next day.)

*God* knows the end from the beginning!

The future will be bright for me and mine.

Jesus told me one evening, "I'm going to be a revelation to the sinners and an inspiration to the saints!"

I long for that day!

# Back Seat in Motion

No, I'm not talking about your significant other. I'm talking about what happened to me when I trusted the people I left home with. Let me start at the beginning.

When I was at my mom's house at age twenty, I couldn't find a job, so I found this ad in the Lake Charles American Press stating, "Come travel and have fun selling books and magazines."

The word *travel* caught my eyes, so I called my mom's friend to give me a ride to the Candlelight Motel for an interview. I met two white girls. They were all bubbly and joyous, telling me how much fun I'm going to have if I come with them. Gloria and I left to go home and pack; meanwhile, Gloria called my mom behind me, getting ready to do.

We call our mother Ma. She came home early because of the phone call. When she got home, Ma stood in the bedroom doorway and raised hell. She was yelling at me, so the more she yelled, the more clothes I put in my big green suitcase. I called Gloria again to take me to the Candlelight Inn.

When she pulled off, all these men were coming out of the motel, and there was no sign of the bubbly girls. A feeling came over me like none other. I was afraid I didn't have any change to call home, and on top of that, I didn't think they would have let me. When everybody got in the car, they made sure I was in the middle of the back seat. We headed west, and I knew I had to pass by my house from the freeway, but I couldn't jump out. My heart fell to my knees. I knew it was no turning back. we stopped in Galveston, Texas, at the beach for two days, then we headed to Houston, Texas. I remember we all went to a club called The Pink Elephant, then we checked into a remote, out-of-the-city-limits motel. Upon retiring for the night, I noticed someone had gone through my suitcase. I became very uncomfortable.

I didn't say anything to any. I just went to bed early. The next day, which was Monday morning, we had to begin our day first with breakfast, then go out in pairs to knock on people's doors requesting that they buy the various magazines and TV guides for a small reasonable price, promising them their order will be in two weeks. We take the money, knowing that's a lie. The boss man was pocketing all of it. After three weeks of the nonsense, I asked the head man if I could go home. He told me yes, then he asked me to be his girlfriend.

I told him no, so you know that didn't sit well with him. I went to my room. I lay with my face to the wall. Around nine o'clock, a white couple came into the room, asking for me. She said I was sleeping, but I wasn't. The man said, "The boss told us to sleep in front of the door just in case I have any bright ideas about escaping."

My stomach became nausea I caught the biggest headache of my life. Even if I were to run away, the motel was in a deserted, remote area. Early the next morning, around 1:00 a.m., everybody had to get up and head out. I purposely left behind a purse with my name and my mom's phone number. The car they put me in was a 1964 Ford Galaxie 500.

I was in the back seat alone. The driver was white, and the front passenger was black. He drove and drove. Not one time I knew where I was. Everything they did was secretive.

I don't know what time it was, but we stopped for lunch. I didn't eat. I was too nervous. After lunch back, from the back seat, all I can see all around me in front of me were all kinds of trucks—big, little, and huge. My imagination was very perplexed.

After a while, while driving south, we all heard this loud horn. So we three people in the car all looked to the left. It was a Pinto truck with my big green suitcase tied on top of the car while the driver took the exit in front of him. Then later that day, a beige Cadillac passed by my window, so I can see a doll that was covered in something red that represented blood sitting in the back window. By that time, I was enormously afraid and paranoid. In my mind, I just knew I was going to be a sex slave somewhere far away.

I didn't have any time on me. I knew it was late in the evening, and the car needed gas. This was my chance. I thought before we got to the gas station, the black passenger turned around and told me, "If you don't want to find your ass in the trash can, you better not say anything."

I swallowed my tongue. The very, very old, slim, wrinkled man stared me hard in the face. He could see I was asking for his help with my countenance, yet he looked away and asked, "May I help you?" to the driver. I must say when we went back to the cars after lunch, a young white boy was placed in the back seat with me. He was very talkative.

When the driver said his talking kept me from being in the state they wanted me to be in they, took him away. "God keeps telling me he had a snake around his neck, but my Father didn't let me see that." After getting gas, they drove for hours and hours, no green signs anywhere to tell me where I was. It felt like it could have been 9:00 or 10:00 p.m. The driver of the car drove into this motel parking lot. It was filled with men and women. Black and white were all on one accord, chanting something in unison. I couldn't understand what they were saying at that time. That was the straw that broke the camel's back. The driver saw that I was leaning toward the back left door, slobbering. He quickly drove me to another large parking lot, jumped from the wheel, opened my back door, and quickly threw me on the cold parking lot and fled, leaving me in a fetal position.

Later on, a man came out of this very large building. I can hear him, but I can't see him. He kept asking my name and where I come from. I couldn't and wouldn't answer because I thought those sets of people were the same ones who responded to me being there. I don't know what happened to me, and I don't know how long I stayed in that large building. I didn't trust anyone. I thought they wanted me dead too.

I wasn't too cooperative with anything, but they did whatever they had to do to get me well. I never forgot my phone number at my mom's house or my name out of the clear blue sky. While a nurse was babysitting me, I blurted out, "Can someone take your money out of the bank without your signature?" She answered no. But my mom found a way to do it. I told the nurse, "I want to call my mom." The doctor dialed the number, and when we heard each other's voice, we both wept.

Then the doctor asked the nurse to take me out of the office so he could talk to my mom.

God forgive me for thinking about money when I first came to my senses. That was foolish. To God be the glory. In my life, I said that because I had five hundred dollars in the bank from job corps.

The day the nurse came to get me because my mom was there to come get me. She placed me in a room, but the room was empty. I immediately thought someone was playing a trick on me. I guess the doctor wanted to see how I was going to react in the empty room, then the second door opened in the room.

My mom was very tall when she opened the second door in the room. I saw a white-and-gold light silhouetted her six-foot frame. I hugged my mom so tight. When I saw her, I saw Jesus.

She talked with the doctor, and he told her when she got me home to take me to the mental clinic for further treatment. I've been going ever since. When we were in the car, Ma kept asking Maudrey, "Them people fed you?" I told her I was scared of people. I didn't trust anyone. I didn't know I was in a hospital no matter how many white coats were there.

As the driver, my mom paid to come get me. The Holy Spirit whispered to me to turn around, so I turned around. I saw the big bronze sign that said "Norman Oklahoma Mental Hospital." That's where the kidnappers brought me from Houston, Texas. That's not all. Early one morning, my mom was getting ready to take me to the mental clinic, but she forgot something in the house. While she was in the house, one of the kidnappers jumped out of his car and yelled my name and said, "We coming back for you." My house was right next to the Enterprise Boulevard exit.

I never told anyone because I know they would think just another thing in my mental mind. Well, I lived in fear for decades until one day God himself told me he was not going to let anyone take me again.

By the way, my mom fed me steak and potato wedges for a long time. I can't explain why my sickness lasted so long. I know sometimes I forgot to take my medicine. There were times when I did take my medicine, I got sick. I know I couldn't fight the devil in my own strength.

That's why I sold out to God. I'm sorry if I offended anyone. Blame my mind, not my heart. I don't know what the kidnappers did to me. Only God Jesus and the Holy Spirit will be able to explain my condition to everyone, even myself, in the movie.

It was a T-shirt I bought from Walmart one time said, "I can explain it to you but I can't make you understand it."

The only motion that was on the back seat of the car were evil spirits in my mind such as fear, paranoia, and devilish imagination! That's what they raped.

## MAUDREY ZENON

I bought a T-shirt at Walmart one day. It said, "I can explain it but I can't make you understand! the reality of it all."

# *Don't Let the Devil Fool You Suicide Is Not the Answer!*

I wrote this story before, so I'm going to give you a condensed form.

In the spirit of the holidays, I met this man on a blind date. When I got in the car, I thought he was goofy-looking because he had on some gold-rimmed eyeglasses. When he spoke to me, I didn't think much of him. The girls sat in the back seat and the men in the front seat. When we got to the club, it had a foyer. We were in one corner of the room, and the men were in another corner. The lights were bright, then I saw the most handsome man I ever met. He had taken off those stupid glasses and left them in the car. He had the most beautiful brown eyes, big and mesmerizing; long, firm legs and arms; and a beautiful smile. It was love at first sight. Most of all, he was a dancer and a talker. We became friends, but it was short-lived. We went to the movies a lot. I remember the first one: *Cornbread, Earl and Me.*

I had a two-bedroom house. He didn't come over that much. I just thought school was keeping him away. We had made plans to go to the Tuesday night discount night movie, but that didn't happen. He came over all right not to be with me but to break up with me. He was living with a woman, but I didn't know it because he talked about living with me. I'll never forget it was a Tuesday night when he left. It rained cats and dogs on a loud stormy night. I was so devastated. I wanted to die. I thought, *I'll do something easy. I'll turn on the gas from the heater.* My mind was made up, but much to my surprise Jesus spoke to my heart. He said, "Maudrey, didn't I show you the family loves you?"

"Yes, God," I cried out. "I'm sorry."

That's how I know he stops everyone from committing such a despicable act; it all depends on which voice you're listening to.

We are all made in the image of God; he knows when it's time to give up the spirit within. The Bible says we can live a long satisfying life in love, holiness, and righteousness!

# I Don't Mind Telling You! 'Cause I Love You

Some readers may ask, "Why is she telling all her business?" Number one, they are all covered by the blood of *Christ*, and that's what I want for you. "Stop the sin, and win with Jesus." I'm not doing anything that the preachers of old used to ask everyone not to do. Now the majority of them are just preaching about "prosperity."

That's all well and dandy, but the wages of sin is still death! That want to get you in heaven! I can't emphasize enough: you must repent, be sorry for your sins, ask Jesus to come inside your heart to live and guide, be baptized (dunked) in water, then live holy each day to the fullest to the best of your ability with the Holy Spirit! Let me not forget.

You must be baptized in the spirit with the utterance of speaking in tongues, the evidence of it. Amen.

# *To God Be the Glory*
# *Houston, Texas*

In the summer of 1974, I was working in a bar as a waitress. I brought this particular customer his drink. He spoke to me, and I replied, then he asked me if he could walk me home after my shift. First of all, I didn't live within walking distance, so I kindly told him no thank you. He asked the same question again, and I gave the same answer by the third time. He got furious with me and demanded that it will be so. By that time I'm angry with him. One word after another was said. I don't know how we winded up outside. I was cussing him out big time. Before I knew it, bullets were fired at my feet, about five of them. The next thing I knew, the woman who owned the club was shoving me into her car.

The bullets didn't scare me; they just made me jump back. When I got home, where it was quiet, I realized I could have been killed. Foolishness. Every time I told that testimony, I would always say he shot at my feet. One day in 2006, God spoke to me, "Maudrey, for decades I let you say the gunman shot at your feet. Don't you know my angel stood between you and the bullets? That's why he was so angry. He knew it wasn't supposed to be a miss."

I repented to the Lord, and the next day my love for him was at a deeper depth! By the way, the gunman had just gotten out of the penitentiary, so he probably felt he didn't have much to lose, but I was pregnant and didn't know it!

# Dear Heavenly Father

My one and only grandson, Messiah Christian Zeno,n was taken out of my arms when he was four months old. The mother gave him to a gay couple to raise. Ms. Speight promised me I can have a relationship with him while she has him. Well, she never looked back at me since day one. She took good care of him, no question about that. I only got to see a few pictures on the cell phone until Ms. Speight cut my granddaughter off Facebook. I'm not mad at Ms. Speight. I know she probably felt it was going to be some drama if she would have driven to Lake Charles, Louisiana, at my house, especially if his daddy would have been around.

She would be right. All I want now is to be in his life. He's eight years young now. I don't want him to grow up confused about mommy and mommy. I hope someone straightened that out for Messiah. He resides in Houston, Texas.

Jesus, help me and him come together real soon!

## About the Author

I'm a devout Christian woman who loves God because he saved me from many mishaps, and I'm very grateful for all he has done for me physically, spiritually, and mentally.

Printed in the USA
CPSIA information can be obtained
at www.ICGtesting.com
LVHW040440091024
793337LV00001B/179

9 798887 934334